Selected Works by Lawrence Ferlinghetti

LAWRENCE FERLINGHETTI

OPEN EYE,
OPEN HEART

A NEW DIRECTIONS BOOK

ACKNOWLEDGMENTS

Grateful thanks are given to the editors and publishers of the various pub-
lications in which many of the poems in this book first appeared: *Antaeus,
Bastard Angel, The Berkeley Barb, Big Sky, Bulletin from Nothing, Cafe
Solo, The Carolina Quarterly, Chelsea Review, Choice, El Corno Emplu-
mado, East Village Other, Evergreen Review, Isis, Liberation, Mediter-
ranean Review, The Montreal Gazette, New Directions in Prose and Poetry,
The Nation, The New York Times Book Review, The New York Quarterly,
Pomegranate Broadsides, San Francisco Chronicle, San Francisco Phoenix,
Second Coming, The Sunday Paper, Tansy, Transatlantic Review,
The Village Voice.*

Manufactured in the United States of America
First published clothbound (ISBN: 0-8112-0488-x) and as New Directions
Paperbook 361 (ISBN: 0-8112-0489-8) in 1973
Published simultaneously in Canada by McClelland & Stewart, Ltd.

New Directions Books are published for James Laughlin
by New Directions Publishing Corporation,
333 Sixth Avenue, New York 10014

CONTENTS

I. Open Eye, Open Heart

II. Poems in Transit

III. Public & Political Poems

IV. American Mantra & Songs

Open Eye, Open Heart

TRUE CONFESSIONAL

I was conceived in the summer of Nineteen Eighteen
(or was it Thirty Eight)
when some kind of war was going on
but it didn't stop two people
from making love in Ossining that year
I like to think on a riverbank in sun
on a picnic by the Hudson
as in a painting of the Hudson River School
or up at Bear Mountain maybe
after taking the old Hudson River Line
paddlewheel excursion steamer
(I may have added the paddlewheel—
the Hudson my Mississippi)
And on the way back she
already carried me
inside of her
I lawrence ferlinghetti
wrought from the dark in my mother long ago
born in a small back bedroom—
In the next room my brother heard
the first cry,
many years later wrote me—
"Poor Mom—No husband—No money—Pop dead—
How she went through it all—"
Someone squeezed my heart
to make it go
I cried and sprang up
Open eye open heart where
do I wander
I cried and ran off
into the heart of the world
Carried away

by another I knew not
And which of me shall know my brother?
'I am my son, my mother, my father,
I am born of myself
my own flesh sucked'
And someone squeezed my heart
to make me go
And I began to go
through my number
I was a wind-up toy
someone had dropped wound-up
into a world already
running down
The world had been going on
a long time already
but it made no difference
It was new it was like new
i made it new
i saw it shining
and it shone in the sun
and it spun in the sun
and the skein it spun
was pure light
My life was made of it
made of the skeins of light
The cobwebs of Night
were not on it
were not of it
It was too bright
to see
too luminous
to cast a shadow
and there was another world
behind the bright screens
I had only to close my eyes

for another world to appear
too near and too dear
to be anything but myself
my inside self
where everything real
was to happen
in this place which still exists
inside myself
and hasn't changed that much
certainly not as much
as the outside
with its bag of skin
and its 'aluminum beard'
and its blue blue eyes
which see as one eye
in the middle of the head
where everything happens
except what happens
in the heart
vajra lotus diamond heart
wherein I read
the poem that never ends

MOCK CONFESSIONAL

Fish-sky at morning
and why should I
tell the world about it
It's not the kind of news
makes headlines down here
Anyway I hear people are wondering about me
and I've written this to clear the air
especially since
people who read my books
don't read other books
I'm sometimes known as the creator
of the immortal line
'When I was a boy I was my father'
I generally feel like kissing someone
when I'm asleep
I don't like sweet wine and cigarettes
police and bitchy women
Otherwise I'm amenable
to what goes down out here
I know I'll never amount to anything
I don't want to amount to
which is not to say I'm without ambition
Sometimes I feel a fluttering in me
and I may sometime fly into the sun
wearing wax wings
I have a feeling I'm falling
on rare occasions
but most of the time I have my feet on the ground
I can't help it if the ground itself is falling
I sometimes wonder what my totem animal is
In any case I'm not a crow or a grey fox
I may be somewhere between a centaur

and Sancho Panza's ass
I know a good thing when I see it
and intend to survive
even if it means being a survivor
I have strange dreams sometimes
but they're not half as weird as
what I see walking down the street
I never did like people who walk like
they're on their way to a party
When I'm at cocktail parties
I usually don't say what I'm thinking
which results in the usual drunkenness
I can't help it if Catholic priests
won't accept my confession
that I consider the Immaculate Conception
a cock-and-bull story
and always viewed the world as a *mons veneris*
After all Father
there must have been plans
for more than two Comings
If this sounds like bright cocktail chatter
remember I'm drinking out of desperation
I believe in the Revolution
in its double-edged image
but baby yours is not mine
I refuse to confess to the boys
or the ladies in the bathroom
What could they be up to
which I am not up to
Why don't we all just dance and sing
and let the appendages hang out where they will
Let's forge on to simpler things
The last time I saw Paris
was in the winter of 1967
when I had to sleep in a windowless room

in a street whose name I'd rather not remember
since I insisted in staying in the same hotel
I'd stayed in as a student a century ago
which now was made over into a mattress factory
Some days I just don't know what to make of things
Other days I'm sure I have the solution to everything
the little key that will fit everything
and turn everything to my own alchemy
if not the wooden key that mayors give you
Well I'll have to begin again
It seems my personal life is a complete fuck-up
though I'm a raving success in the field
While I'm catching the high fly
a worm has succeeded in eating
a hole in my soul
When I reach down to mend it
I find a cocoon in my crotch
which becomes a butterfly as I watch
While I'm zipping up
it flits to my heart
And the world begins again
With a lurch it starts whirling once more
with its little supercargo of flesh
The race horses in their slots
take off again
but the big board registers Tilt
when someone like the government
jiggles the machine
As I was saying it seems
I'm a complete failure on the home-front
and my key won't fit my own door anymore
but that's still no sign I'm not an artistic triumph
I've proved that already with my fearless pen
though now it may run dry
and I have to dip it in some body fluid to continue

of which there are only two symbolic choices:
blood or water
The moving finger writes in both
and fumbles on
but leaves its indelible traces
only in one
which makes me wonder
if I really choose to be immortal
Excuse me for a moment
There's another butterfly
lighted on my fly
and my metamorphosis
may not be done
though now I am 'old'
and am my son

IN A TIME OF REVOLUTION
FOR INSTANCE

I had just ordered a fishplate at the counter when
three very beautiful
fucked-up people entered
I don't know how or why I
thought they must be
fucked-up except
they were very beautiful
two men and one very
beautiful goldenhaired
young woman very
well groomed and
wearing sports clothes like
as if they must have
just gotten out of an
old-fashioned Stutz
roadster with top
down and tennis rackets and
the woman strode to the back
of the restaurant
found a vacant table and
strode back and
got the other two
beckoning with elegant
gestures and
smiling slightly at them and
the three of them
walked back slowly to the table
as if they were not afraid
of anything or anyone
in that place and
took possession of it with

lovely expressions and
the very lovely young lady
settled herself so easily
on the settee beside
the younger of the two men
both of whom had
lightbrown wavy hair not too long
and cut like Hollywood
tennis stars or anyway
like visitors from some other town more
elegant than our own and
they were obviously so much better
looking and so much better
brought up than anyone else
in the place
they looked like they might be
related to the Kennedys and
they obviously had no Indian or Eyetalian
blood in them
and she obviously with
so many avenues open to her
with her two men
one of whom could have been
her brother
I could not imagine her *carrying*
a carbine and
she kept tossing her hair ever so gently out
of her eyes and
smiling at both of them and
at nothing in particular that I
could imagine and
her lips were moving gently with
her gentle smile and
I kept trying to imagine what
she could possibly be saying with

11

those perfect lips over
those perfect teeth so white
with her eyes now and then sliding
over and down the counter where
a lot of little people sat
quietly eating their quite ordinary
lunches while
the three beautiful people who
could have been anywhere
seemed just about to order
something special and
eat it with ice cream and cigarettes and
my fish finally arrived looking
not quite unfrozen and
quite plastic but
I decided to eat it anyway
she was a beautiful creature and I
felt like Charlie Chaplin eating his shoe
when her eyes slid over me
the Modern Jass Quartet
came over the Muzak speakers and
under other circumstances
in a time of revolution for instance
she might have fucked me

THE ASTONISHED HEART

She of the shining eyes
in the next booth
Ramada Inn Lawrence Kansas
Beautiful teeth and long hair
talking to a smiler in sharkskin
She is twenty and aglow
saying something important
about their life together
It must be serious
the way she looks at him
with her far-eyed look
half-smiling
or maybe it is just about the tragedy
of some movie she's just been to
I can't hear the words
Just the voice lisping a little
flat almost
except for the eyes
He smiles into them
They are both smiling
into each other
Maybe it is just a little joke
between them
not a tragedy at all
There is nothing to do about it
in either case
Just watch it happen
amazed and aghast
at the fantastic craziness of it
and of existence
which just goes on
bowling us over

Set 'em up in the other alley
Wow watch this one
I got my crystal spectacles on
Soon soon their supper will come
Soon soon they will eat it
or each other
not necessarily a tragedy
She is giving him her
long look again
Soon the curious plastic-antique restaurant
will curl up around them
and blow away with them
over the plains of Kansas
not necessarily
an ecological tragedy
Maybe it is all just a goofy movie
about eating
He may be about to eat a fish
whose baked eye glares up at him
Soon soon they will devour each other
Eyes feasting on each other
each prepares the other's surrender
Soon she will look away
with her long look
out a window
through the Standard Station's neons
toward the plains
where somewhere soon
they will lie together hot
under the sun at noon
Soon soon she will finish eating
her appetizer
Soon soon she will look at him again
You can tell she's still hungry
Woman is a wonderful invention

of man
And man a wonderful invention
of woman
Soon soon they will be born again in the sun
Soon too soon they will be wonderfully done
with each other
She looks away from him now
into the great American night
and seems to see very far
unless it's just contact lenses
making her eyes
so shiny
There is a great crowded bluff
in Lawrence Kansas
that looks a long way
into the astonished heart
of America

SUEÑO REAL

1.

In the eternal dream-time
                    a fish dreamt ocean
                    a bird sky
And I stand on the beach in the land
        where all is still frontier
And hold an aluminum bird in my hand
And don't dream sand
                    running through my head
                            as through an hourglass

2.

In the eternal dream-time
    a sigh
            falls from the sky
    from some other history than our own
                    as if the world were almost
                        brand new

3.

Ah, como la tierra es buena
    y la vida—
            la vida es un sueño real . . .
Sun on fire
            sucked into ocean
        And the only shadow
                    the shadow of desire afire

4.

                        In the eternal dream-time

a whale of a man
           in a great round
                      Mexican sombrero
      with a wide-open
              painted eye on it
suddenly appears
          on the beach by the woods
    The sun
         casts its shadow
                 on the ground

5.

Back at the cabin in the woods by the stream
    the white copy of Venus Aphrodite
      stands silent on the porch
  Silk cobwebs on her
         glisten and quiver in wind
           lyre-strands strung
              from head to shoulder
The stream below
                sheds its multi-murmuring
   A million
        spirit-voices
       undertone to birds
           in lush trees above
   A bee browses
         on the alabaster breasts
      and moves
          to the very mouth of Venus
      who is no longer a copy
Ah, aaah
     the universe breathes
A bat
   scrunches up
         under the eaves

6.

Loony surrealist dream
    of a lead soldier in a
                tin cowboy hat
      riding over
          the burnt horizon
         backwards on his horse
In his hand he holds
           a small white horse
        bearing a small white cowboy
               between its teeth
And this cowboy is singing
           'Life is a real dream'

7.

And I went out in the dark dawn
  in the morning of the world
    in the first morning
      and saw the Northern Cross
      with a slow thrust
        bury itself in the mountain
          and burn there in white fire
    huge Excalibur
         stuck in stone

8.

What is that bird
         trying to call my attention?
I've been fifty years
       waiting for this moment
         of light
  And he took it

9.

I know that I don't dream
    'Life
        dreams me'
It is life
    that dreams around me
The leaves breathe
        the hills
          breathe
There is a willow aflame
        with sun
There are a series
      of waterproof mouths
And my words are
      myself. . . .

10.

Transliteration of inanimate objects
    into real beings . . .
        a palimpsest
          an illegible
            manuscreed
        Braille
          night-thought spoke
by a stream impossible
        to decipher. . . .

BIG SUR GRASS REVERIE

Everything reduced to its essence deduced from its essentials
and I have a choice between laughing & weeping
A bee buzzes in my guitar A burro brays up the canyon of time
A dog adrift unwinds its tail in eternity A tail turned to a
crank turns out barks
And a lovely galloping pony on the wall in my small daughter's
drawing shakes its long mane and becomes my daughter
ready for slaughter A child's play is her first attempt at
living & loving
And a girl walking down the steep high road through the trees
awake becomes a walking fertility root with brown breasts
and legs attached to the earth lush brown goddess darling
take me
And a fat man remains a fat mannikin in a magazine but is also
a ball-bearing baboon ashake with laughter after a fuck
And a tall man walking is a walking phallus in a kingdom of
clitori afire afloat on a stream long hair streaming & the
lips singing Byebye Now I am not mad The end is just be-
ginning and all is tragic with joy

FUGITIVE CONFIGURATIONS

Fugitive configurations
figures on a distant cliff
                    our bodies soon
                        all blown away
    all transitory all imaginary
                graceless
                            stuttering
Nothing exists
                beyond nothing
        We are
            Nothing
                    but ephemera scribbled
        on a distant landscape
                brushed away
light out of light
                flickered
                        I
                long to look
                    in your eyes—
                            imaginary one
                                transitory being

        Crickets wake me
                out of that deep
        I rise and look
                    over the sea
                in first morning
                It
                    is a great grey eye
                        pearl pupil
                                glimmering
                opening & closing
                            its lace
                        eyelashes

We constantly
              wake to a dream
              deeper than sleep
Figures
         on a cliff erased
    Lips upon the beach
                              washed out
        Sea's mouth
                   yawning utters
              Ocean's long withdrawing OM
They
     are swimming through it
   They
       are surfing in it
                         through the lashes
    They
        are drowning in it
                              Panic ephemera
               ah ah the
                    skillful yachts
                         still pass over
    Eye winks
           open
               Oh
                 I
                   am open
                       I look
                       into the grey deeps

                            dark dark

         I look
              into your eyes
                              imaginary woman

THE REAL MAGIC OPERA BEGINS

In our tatami room
                    our Sacred Jar of Life
        stands full of silence
                            full of light
        in the still white air
And all our 'gods'
                    are silent
                        They
                    have nothing more to say
                        to any of us
                        assembled here

What else what else
                    to be aware of
                        with our 'expanded consciousness'
                        and our 'total awareness'

And how much more Reality
                            is there to be aware of
            is there for us to grin and bear?

My autoharp
            has no answer
        nor any further need to sing

Daniel Moore's Tibetan horn
                            stands echoing
                        and no longer wails
                            ragas of ecstasy
                            ragas of despair
                    in the still white air

And a lovely Japanese platter
   presented to me by the father
     of a young dead Sansei friend
       stands upright on its stand in light
       silent as he is silenced
             in the silent air
             of night

Incense stand stands smokeless
Bronze vajra lies all still
      floating lotus petals shut
          on pure Nothingness
     above which
          dead brilliant butterflies
       hang pinned up very high
   with nowhere else to fly
         nowhere else to die

Silent Shiva dances still
   inside a silent wheel
     with extra arms akimbo

And a hanging seed scroll symbol
   still receives its flying seed of light
     in the wind which speaks of life
     where we have thought to be
             very high

As the light falls on earth
  on us assembled here
As the light falls like silence itself
          which is light
   And the freaked-out wind
      stops howling
      through the high passes

And the still rain starts falling—
 the soft still rain
  the soft voice of rain
   sweet voice of rain
     on summer grasses
   on a lighted mesa
     very high up
      very far away

And the lotus floats free
    in the rain of pure light

And the real magic opera begins

STONE REALITY MEDITATION

Humankind can indeed bear
very much reality
That 'busy little monster
                                manunkind'
can bear it too
So may womankind
So can every kind
of clay and creature
Trees too can bear it
after the leaves have flown away
after the birds have blown away
'bare ruined choirs' bear it
as stones do
They too bear the 'heavy weight
of creation'
as we do
cast in clay and stoned in earth
Masters of ecstasy

SUNRISE, BOLINAS

This little heart that remembers
                    every little thing
        begins the day
                    most of the time
                        by an attempt at singing
                            some sunny rhyme

Such effrontery, such audacity
                    in the face of everything!
Still I'll sing at the sun
                    for a beginning—

Such presumption, such perversity
                        to mistake bird-cries for song
                            when they may really be
                                cries of despair!
        As if our life
            as if all life
                were not a tragedy
                    though all is passing fair

        As if our life
                    were not so very various
                        as to turn it all to litany—

O drunk flute
                O Golden Mouth
                            sing a mad song
                                    to save us

SONG OF LOVE & DESIRE

(After E. A. Poe)

Love is the strangest bird
that ever winged about the world
and whirled and flashed at us
                              its dark marked wings
And stranger still
the image of the loved one
that gestures through our sleep
and drifts from us
through every crowd and cloud
and shift of season
O dark of hair
In sleep we see her body singing half aloud
its alabaster song
We see the parted lips
We hear the muteless voice
struck through the so-called "sad études
of human reason"
Dark of hair O dark of hair
désir délire
desire lost and dreaming
Thy so-called classic face
Thy so-called naiad airs
do make me roam

PLEASE, ETERNAL WOMAN, DON'T...

Now that we have examined your lips
O Eternal Woman
and decided why the curve
of the lower lip smiling
or mouth half-open
should dispel the world
at a glance
or make sleepwalkers dance
in ecstasy
or abandonment
as if some god
or some other bedazzlement
were to say
'That is not what I meant
that is not what I meant to build at all
when I made that firmament
of flesh'
as if
as if sweet love were all
there was to think of
whereas those lips
were only meant to drink of
sweet *amer*
and merriment
with no provision for
what they might touch and kiss
or graze upon
or otherwise enmesh
Please, eternal woman,
do not lead me on & on
to that mad point at which
when you might say 'I love you'

29

I would have to say
               'Say something kind instead'
or simply wish
               yes deeply wish
                    that I were dead
and so forever after call
               all love a plague
               all love a dread contagion
For it is not
          O it is not—
    so long as you
               so long as you—
                    Ah, well!—
                    There is no answer in
                    my mandolin

AT KENNETH REXROTH'S

Sweet William Blake
                    in a book in Santa Barbara
          echoes
                    in the eucalyptus

★

I roll seven chopsticks together
     and in their clicking hear
the sound of last summer's cicadas

★

I look Westward
                    into the end of day
     The Last Frontier
                         still made of Water

A PHOENIX AT FIFTY

At new age fifty
turn inward on old self
and rock on my back in a torn green hammock
deep in a ruined garden
where first the sweet birds sang
behind a white wood cottage
at Montecito Santa Barbara
sunk in sea-vine succulents
under huge old eucalyptrees
wind blows white sunlight thru
A mute ruined statue of a nymph dancing
turns in sun
as if to sing 'When day is done'
It is not
A helicopter flies
out of an angle of the sun
its windmill choppers waving
thru the waving treetops
thru which the hot wind blows & blows
pure desire made of light
I float on my back in the sea of it
and gaze straight up into eye-white sky
as into eyes of one beloved whispering
   'Let
     me
      in'
Too bright
   too bright!
I close my eyes
lest sun thru such lenses
set me afire

but the blown light batters thru
lids and lashes
I burn and leave
no ashes

Yet will arise

THE MAN WHO RODE AWAY

(To D. H. Lawrence)

Above Taos now
                    I peer through the crack
        of your locked door
                    Dead Lawrence
and there indeed I see
                    they've got you now at last
        safely stashed away
                    locked away from the light
        of your dear sun
                    in the weird great dark
            of your little
                    shuttered shrine
with the dark brown cover
                    of your old portable
clenched like a jaw upon
                    dumb keys
                        teeth sans tongue
            as in a mute mask
                    of a Greek megaphone

        Ah here's real proof
                    the soul has its rages—
            dampered!
                    in darkness!
        shrine locked—
                    booby-trapped for burglars—
plumed serpent stoned
                    into a gargoyle!

Lawrence Lawrence bearded David
                              Phoenix flamed
        out of a mine-head
                        ash to ash
            Sown in Venice
                        and resown in America
                (del Norte)
                            Where now
                here now
                            your portable seed
            has blown away
                            Other seeds
                are growing
                            Not yours
                Lawrence
                        in the white sands
                                proving grounds!

Lawrence now I see you come alone
from your cribbed cabin
all fenced in the backyard compound
of that big caretaker's house

You stand still a moment in the still air.

Your eyes have a Mexican look
turned South
over the arroyos
ahora y siempre

Winter is coming

You have your ticket

You have your blue denim jacket

You have your crazy Stetson

Your tin phoenix tacked to a tree
drops in a giftshop window

A mistral wind
rattles the pine needles
of your bones

AN ELEGY ON THE DEATH
OF KENNETH PATCHEN

A poet is born
A poet dies
And all that lies between
                              is us
                              and the world

And the world lies about it
    making as if it had got his message
        even though it is poetry
but most of the world wishing
    it could just forget about him
        and his awful strange prophecies

Along with all the other strange things
    he said about the world
        which were all too true
            and which made them fear him
                more than they loved him
                    though he spoke much of love
Along with all the alarms he sounded
    which turned out to be false
        if only for the moment
all of which made them fear his tongue
    more than they loved him
Though he spoke much of love
        and never lived by 'silence exile & cunning'
            and was a loud conscientious objector to
                the deaths we daily give each other
                    though we speak much of love

And when such a one dies
    even the agents of Death should take note
        and shake the shit from their wings
                                        in Air Force One
    But they do not
                        And the shit still flies
And the poet now is disconnected
                            and won't call back
    though he spoke much of love

And still we hear him say
                'Do I not deal with angels
                    when her lips I touch'
And still we hear him say
                'O my darling troubles heaven
                    with her loveliness'
And still we love to hear him say
    'As we are so wonderfully done with each other
    We can walk into our separate sleep
    On floors of music where the milkwhite cloak
                of childhood lies'
And still we hear him saying
        'Therefore the constant powers do not lessen.
        Nor is the property of the spirit scattered
        on the cold hills of these events'
And still we hear him asking
        'Do the dead know what time it is?'

He is gone under
                He is scattered
                                undersea
        and knows what time
                - but won't be back to tell it
    He would be too proud to call back anyway
        And too full of strange laughter
                    to speak to us anymore anyway

And the weight of human experience
        lies upon the world
     like the chains of the sea
                  in which he sings
And he swings in the tides of the sea
    And his ashes are washed
             in the tides of the sea
And 'an astonished eye looks out of the air'
          to see the poet singing there

And dusk falls down a coast somewhere

   where a white horse without a rider
       turns its head
           to the sea

*First read at the City Lights Poets Theatre Kenneth Patchen
Memorial Reading, February 3, 1972, San Francisco*

POEM FOR OLD WALT

SPRING DUSK DARK SHORE
LONG ISLAND NEW YORK APRIL
SKY OVER PATCHOGUE DENSE & GREY
AS WHITMAN'S BEARD
FLIGHTS OF GREY GEESE
NESTED IN IT
OVER HULK OF HIS FAIR BODY—
'FISH-SHAPE PAUMANOK'—
HULK OF HIM HOVE-TO
OFF OLD MANNAHATTA—
POETS STILL
SWIM OFF OF IT
THEIR FAR CRIES FAILING
LIKE LOST SAILORS IN A BURNING
TURNER SHIPWRECK
RED SUN FLAMES THROUGH
ON THE VERY SHORES OF LIGHT!

Poems in Transit

INTO DARKNESS, IN GRANADA

O if I were not so unhappy
I could write great poetry!
Dusk falls through the olive trees
Federico García Lorca
leaps about among them
dodging the dark as it falls upon him
O if only I could leap like him
and make great songs
Instead I swing about wildly
as in a children's
jungle gym
in a vacant lot by Ben Shahn
jump up suddenly
upon the back of a running horse
in the face of a plains' twister
And paddle away slowly
into total darkness
in a Dove boat

A GIACOMETTI SUMMER

Walking thru the Giacometti exhibition
                                        love's bodies lost
                    London, summer, 'sixty-five
where are they going
                        those strange standing figures
metal shadows of themselves
                                    tall as stone trees
    and too thin to have hearts

And where then am i going
                            with my fat meat
I do not have such huge feet
                            for pedestals
to keep me from falling over
                            unbalanced

Cave-light slants down on me
                            thru the bone sky
Black shadows bend those bodies
                                where love hangs heavy

Stone face gawks down on me
                            inchoately!

AN IMAGINARY HAPPENING, LONDON

In the lower left-hand corner
of an album landscape
I am walking thru a dark park
with a noted nymphomaniac
trying to discover
for what she is noted

We are talking as we walk
of various villainies
of church & state
and of the tyrannies
of love & hate

The moon makes hairless nudes

An alabaster girl upon her back
becomes a body made of soap
beneath a wet gypsy

Suddenly we rush
thru a bent gate
into the hot grass

One more tree
falls in the forest

LONDON, RAINY DAY

Nothing ever happens
            on rainy mornings like this

Life lopes on down here

Life's eternal situations
               stutter on

Nothing changes nothing sings
Nothing takes wing

Nothing moves in the leaded air

No shadows move
            anywhere
        because there is no shade
         where there is no sun

Even the trees do not move
       even the trees do not turn
          and drop their leaves like wings

The blue rider does not appear

THOUGHTS TO A CONCERTO
OF TELEMANN

'The curious upward stumbling motion
of the oboe d'amore'
must be love itself among the strands
of emotion. It is as if its motion
were not its own at all,
as if these hands
had never struck those strings
we sing to,
swing to
(as puppets do, unbroken)
as if we never really meant to
be so strung to
those sweet pitches
love so frets us to
so tautly
so mutely
(love's bodies laid like harps!)
and then as if
there never were still more
unspoken,
as if dumb mind did never grieve
among the woodwinds,
as if its chords
did never quiver anymore
as in a buried mandolin,
as if that love
were hardly in it
anymore,
nor sounded in it

anymore,
nor heart hear it
nor life bear it
anymore.
Yet it does, it does!

CRO-MAGNONS

Cro-Magnons carried stones for books
And a flat dark stone I came upon
was one in which I read
the carbon copy histories
of creepy man
in the fine print of fossils pressed
between the stone's aged pages
the first syllables of recorded time
made into burning messages
about the first decline and fall
and the dissent of species

so that
when I cracked it open I surprised
the shadow of a lizard on the steps
of an Alexandrian branch library
burning on the broken stone
in a bright daze of sunlight
And in a flicker of that lizard's loose tongue
in one cooled instant of carbonized time
deciphered eternity

SEVERAL SURREALIST LITANIES
FOR A FILM ON THE CEMETERY
OF PÈRE LACHAISE

Ah ah
the dead
Stoned into light
Struck
in glib Te Deums
Rigid virgins
lushed at last
Angry roosts & moults
Vaults of Nothingness!
in hook of time
in ora pro nobis
Dawn's bees turn black
spider stitch
stone tattoo
in brainpan plumbing
lipread in toto
by Seine side faraway
sin side
in night light
in whiteness
laughing
liebfraumilch unbottled
trees dip their creepers hanging
underwater wound
One by one
Where— are— we— going?
groped by gay peckers
in cornhold extremis
Do the dead know

which way they're falling
falling
into lightness
in glove compartments of the moon
green grows our underwear
in diaper dung profundis
The nailed foot falls
the grass lilts wilting
the sylph skin
shuffles off
its glass bottom
bateau mouche
O drunk bateau
brak brak brak
your cold grey stones
that swinging hang below
nested underleg
salt crotch
brackish breakage by the waters of—
blithering sins and daughters of—
in catcall domini
fair frieze of scenery
Gypsy picnickers
Sunday fishers
(What mad pursuit?)
Fair fellow met
Laughing fellow rover
Rose-hip
Blear Moses
Clay somnambule!
O bread-breasted woman
kiss kiss in stone boudoirs
Saboteurs of ourselves!
How have I not seen those dead before
one by one

two by two
Have not seen them
Have been but a muted eye
on them
But I
the Eye must speak
of them
do more than see them all
Beat battlements
engraved!
trees turned to ashfoot bodies
sackbuts sewn in clothing
stashed away in white sidings
in gaudeamus igitur
cricket & violin
old Stradivarius consommé
in Père Lachaise's lap
oh the flies falter eating Love
Finger me not
I'm loose in the vulva
oh we devour ourselves!
See, see, the dead collide alive
the white void sings
leaves turn to toast
the gold ground utters
its autumn
Such seasons, such chateaux!
O sun, white tear
old rockingchair necropolis
hurls us out
through the rock cities
Night Night
rocks us rootless
(Flights of foster souls fly over)
knocks us

rocks us yes
and fingers us
(ah ah tarantula)
The earth is god's greengrocer yes
green daddy dada flocks us footloose
to the Farallones alone
and Night pours out on us
in three rivers
Myself wigged out
in photo clothing. . . .

TOC TOC: A COUPLE OBSERVED

(After Apollinaire)

Without closing its wings
               the plane lands
          its shadow in mourning
                    for itself
          come down to itself on earth
Toc toc the clock in the tower continues
          to cast its shadow
                    onto the airfield
Toc toc another stroke of the feather
          strikes another line
                    in my face
     My shadow in mourning
                    for my self
                    tied to my feet
                    falls out of the plane
                    head first
                    ahead of my fate
Toc toc the shadows in the gardens of Père Lachaise
          draw over Apollinaire's tombeau
Toc toc the flowers of the garden are faded
          loose leaves & aeroplanes blow away
Toc toc another stroke of the feather
                    another line in a face
                    a woman withdraws a man goes off
                    with his shadow
                    withdrawn into himself
                         Toc toc
                    they both turn
                    too late! too late!

TROIS POÈMES SPONTANÉS
SUR LA FORCE DE FRAPPE DE L'AMOUR
À SIX HEURES DU MATIN

I.

Bald musique chauve sourire notre dame of the night streets
dans le trentequarantième de mon âge Quatorze Juillet Caille-
botte Paris toits comme poissons glistening wet and grey sous
la pluie scales into shingles leaves into fishes fuck in the wet
beach of sky poissons se baisant sur les plages-nuages ô notre
seigneur when I rentréd in the dark dawn Cinq Rue Noire
force de frappe sous la fenêtre plus tard où passe la grande
parade de Bastille Day drap noir sinistre illusion Turn Left
phoque-phare strange tank black knight in fishscale armour
drapeau noir strange night en train de se faire en poisson armé
vive-vipère rodant sur les boulevards frappe noire ô elle avait
des grands tétons undone ô somnambule which was myself
imaginaire sweet fille her nerveuse ecstasy joyeuse force flipped
out coming and coming in the deep dawn long ago in the same
street mer glauque gown sur le tapis oh my darling pense pas
love only for we are the baiseurs not the murderers heads
blown bobbing over the sea body lost

in the crowd

II.

Endroits emerveillés nuits partagées rêveries du Night Lunch
solitaire croque-monsieur tortues renversées sous tous les ponts
têtes de tant-pis pieds de cochons bottés sapeurs-pompiers en
train de danser triste valse des plombiers craque-monsieur Love
Your Enemy même La Rousse old Dandelion Head sème à tout
vent pas d'excuse autrement si tu m'amais tu faisais pas comme
ça et sous tous ces ponts de tous ces Mirabeaux coule la vie et il
y a trop de ponts sous lesquels la vie coule ô Inverness ô Mon-
stre de Loch Ness sur toutes les places de la Bastille tournant
et tournant dans la nuit-pas-partagée me sent vachement seul
affreuse tendance de me baiser contre les vitrines but it's all
right Ma dis pas que je vive in a glass house d'Alphaville où on
joue perdant les bateaux mouches font pipi et on danse tou-
jours avec son petit ami six heures du matin yeux fermés Place
Contrescarpe cuisses de couscous

allez

bouffer ensemble

III.

Ceremonial de la vida nuit cassée comme un oeuf in a black bowl the yolk-soleil se lève encore ces croque-notes casqués marchent toujours in the light of it Squads Right le monde takes a turn for the worse Remember the Maine chambered nautilus couldn't turn once it started in any direction et j'suis venu de Spain cet hiver les cloches sonnent toujours et on sait pour qui mais on n'entend plus on danse toujours to dead drums au Café Tambour Place Bastille le bald garçon batte son oeuf sur le comptoir de sa vie casse-croûte the drum-world turns après la pluie plaqué des miroirs brisés où on voit rien que les pieds nus des célébrants figés en éternité figures faces fixed in the dawn stagger onward titubant strung out egg-yolk in the sky et le monde rentre dans l'obscurité du soleil jeu perdant ballon tournant au ciel disparu au-dessus des toits fumés mais l'éclipse des cons va arriver quand même

POUND AT SPOLETO

I walked into a loge in the Teatro Melisso, the lovely Renaissance salle where the poetry readings and the chamber concerts were held every day of the Spoleto Festival, and suddenly saw Ezra Pound for the first time, still as a mandarin statue in a box in a balcony at the back of the theatre, one tier up from the stalls. It was a shock, seeing only a striking old man in a curious pose, thin and long haired, aquiline at 80, head tilted strangely to one side, lost in permanent abstraction. . . . After three younger poets on stage, he was scheduled to read from his box, and there he sat with an old friend (who held his papers) waiting. He regarded the knuckles of his hands, moving them a very little, expressionless. Only once, when everyone else in the full theatre applauded someone on stage, did he rouse himself to clap, without looking up, as if stimulated by sound in a void. . . . After almost an hour, his turn came. Or after a life. . . . Everyone in the hall rose, turned and looked back and up at Pound in his booth, applauding. The applause was prolonged and Pound tried to rise from his armchair. A microphone was partly in the way. He grasped the arms of the chair with his boney hands and tried to rise. He could not and he tried again and could not. His old friend did not try to help him. Finally she put a poem in his hand, and after at least a minute his voice came out. First the jaw moved and then the voice came out, inaudible. A young Italian pulled the mike up very close to his face and held it there and the voice came over, frail but stubborn, higher than I had expected, a thin, soft monotone. The hall had gone silent at a stroke. The voice knocked me down, so soft, so thin, so frail, so stubborn still. I put my head on my arms on the velvet sill of the box. I was surprised to see a single tear drop on my knee. The thin, indomitable voice went on. I went blind from the box, through the back door of it, into the empty corridor of the theatre where they still sat turned to him, went down and out, into the sunlight, weeping. . . .

Up above the town
by the ancient aqueduct
the chestnut trees
were still in bloom
Mute birds
flew in the valley
far below
The sun shone
on the chestnut trees
and the leaves
turned in the sun
and turned and turned and turned
And would continue turning
His voice
went on
and on
through the leaves. . . .

WOODEN RUSSIA STILL

Knock knock on wooden Russia!
I am a white bird drilling holes
in the white wood of your snow.
To the white birches
that stretch across Siberia
from Vladivostok to Blok
I give one more knock.
Who will answer this time?
Are you still there, poet,
Are you still there, brother, anarchist,
Are you still there, under the plow?
These are not Chekhov's cherished cherry trees
that fell down long ago.
This is the eternal *taiga* now
that still stands up against all winds
dark scars upon the bark.

Knock! Knock!

Let the railsplitter
truly awake.

PERPETUAL REVOLUTION

Woke to the sound
of axes in the wood
It could have been
a hundred years ago
Chop! Chop!
Down go the Cherry Trees
And still it means
the end of an era
All comes down
And a good thing too
Let the chips fly
and down it comes
                    the twisted old order
      crash
            into the underbrush

A house-cat
            gets hit by it
            but walks away from it
They
      are the great quietists
                  the arch reactionaries
         the sphinxes
                  that outlive revolutions
It
   shakes itself all over
                  And purrs out its olive blood
                     in the shape of a watch
                        without hands

POEMS FROM
'RUSSIAN WINTER JOURNAL'

1.

In Khabarovsk above the Amur River, a great deserted merry-goround park with empty Ferris wheels, airplane-ride whirli-gigs with little planes with empty cockpits on ends of long booms attached to a central turntable (empty planes stalled high in air), abandoned pavilions & summer esplanades high over the beach and frozen estuary waters, the beach covered with snow, heroic statue of some hero in a greatcoat & boots striding forward with a great hound wolfdog leading him but all fenced in a little snow-covered plot among winter trees full of stiff brown leaves frozen as blown back from the river, great stark winter trees with sharp shadows all through the slope of the Park frozen against bright blue winter sky, frozen park paths through the snow under the trees, and the empty merry-goround with one Red horse missing, and eight heroic busts larger than life in yellow-white stone or plaster stretched along a curved walk with green wooden-slatted benches, snow on stone beards and eyebrows & eyes staring blind over the water, black boats deserted drawn up on the frozen beach below, and factories away in the distance across the water with long thin chimneys smoking, and an abandoned outdoor dance pavilion with small empty stage, and a very-much-larger-than-life eques-trian statue of a mariner striding with telescope in hand above and beyond the eight heroic busts, he too looking seaward, and a small black & white mongrel dog who runs barking at us from a babushka with knotted arteries, and an old old old tall man in greatcoat & fur hat with a thousand wrinkles, and a wood footbridge over a frozen gulley without a stream, and a small round wooden bird-cage-house with wickets ajar through which birds of summer long since flew to return only when the cuckoo cries in the ginko tree at the top of the Park by the great iron gates through which now passes one big wolf shepherd dog embodying Rama Krishna, leading one white-bearded Walt Whitman Khabarovsk anarchist clochard with homemade bomb in pocket, as we pass out through wrought-iron gates facing the great plaza with its pinnacle stone monument to the Soviet Dead and its 100-foot-long six-foot-high white canvas banner in Russian proclaiming 50TH ANNIVERSARY OF THE GREAT OCTOBER REVOLUTION!

And uptown in front of a big café, one young father in grey lamb wool shako & fur-collared coat hurrying along the wide boulevard sidewalk under the municipal trees, carrying one wooden merrygoround horse under his arm upsidedown. . . .

Recipe for Happiness in Khabarovsk or Anyplace:

One grand boulevard with trees
with one grand café in sun
with strong black coffee in very small cups

One not necessarily very beautiful
man or woman who loves you

One fine day

3.

From Baltic to the Sea of Japan the land uniting Orient &
Europe is covered with huge frozen white butterflies—*schmet-
terlings* wing-to-wing over the plains & tundra, piled up like
snowdrifts in the mountain, fluttered under birches of eternal
taiga, falling through high passes, these frozen white butterflies
like the Great White Night itself, pressing down from Arctic
everywhere, Mongol humans raising round heads out of it &
holding up small faded railroad flags at forlorn way stations.
. . . A Red Flag is added seventeen years after the beginning of
our century. . . . Sound of Mongols fucking under white
birches. . . .
In this White Night Country the wood houses may someday be
turned over by enormous Birds, as beasts sigh, rutting, and a
Red winter sun pours blood out of Manchuria. . . .

4. THE OLD REVOLUTION

When the harvest fails in Russia
I am a sailor again
on the Battleship Potemkin
Only the ship is stuck
in Siberian snowfields
frozen wheatfields
the props won't thresh
And there's blood in the drink
I'm on the bridge as if I were admiral
And I'm down in the boiler room
stoking the old fires—
Nothing moves
And yet it won't sink!

MOON SHOT

The song that never ends
                                on & on
La vie en rose
                    and all that
It's a record
                    that's never broken
        Spin! Spin! Turn & turn & turn!
And we're
                going into cassettes
                            which will be still more unending
                            and even reversible
'There is no end of it
                            the voiceless wailing'!
        Oooolala I can hardly stand it
                    Turn me over & play me again
There's a song in my head goes round & round
            like a fucking merrygoround
        the horses going up & down
                    wooden phalluses up & down
                                over the dance floor
The race is on
                between the war horses
    Which war will win
                    We're into the overtime period
        The brass ring flashes by
                            No one can catch it
        And Mother's in the street
                                her brassiere backward

Let's get with it again
Let's get it together at last

Russia & America
Don't shoot down the moon!
There may still be lovers on it
                    sleeping on the dark side
arms around each other
                    turning into light

Vancouver, B. C.

A SPIDER

Spider in the toiletbowl
in Cholula Mexico!
Twice I spied him—
        all head—
            size of a BB-gun pellet—
and so many long legs—
            stiff bent antennae!
Twice he was there
         when I came to drown him
Twice he ducked down the drain
          before the water hit him
   shrunk into nada
            in a dark flash
   convulsed back
         into heart of darkness
   shrunk back into
         bowel of earth
into some stiff bone hand
        that had let it go
        for the moment of a century
   to seek light, or what—
             Bread & Glory!

Public & Political Poems

CONCRETE POLITICS

```
night night night night night night night
night night night night night night night
night night night night night night night
light  light  light  light  light  light  light
light  light  light  light  light  light  light
light  light  light  light  light  light  light
light light light DEATH light light light
light  light  light  light  light  light  light
light  light  light  light  light  light  light
light  light  light  light  light  light  light
night night night night night night night
night night night night night night night
night night night night night night night
```

A PARADE TIRADE

Good night ladies and good night nuns & priests & monks who never march in peace parades Protestants shouldn't protest The holy wars are over The only united crusade a fund drive and good night holy ministers who evict peace groups from their premises Onward christian soldiers and good night good grey soldier and good night sweet prince Kennedy as long as there are guns they will speak telescopically and good night Colonel Cornpone and good night good night sad cop who turned the hoses on a whole generation and flipped later and good night asinine armistice day parades that nobody under 40 believes in Don't laugh You should take them seriously Those big phony scenes which have nothing to do with us & the way we want to live The america of the american legion isn't ours This ain't 1919 Let them march off a cliff somewhere with their obscene side arms & sinister slogans Call out the horse marines & clean up the mess I didn't know they piled it that high You won't get us to run your errands anymore But here comes the band anyway A catch in the throat A lady liberty on a float God save our country's flag she said and god knows Veterans love wars Their eyes have seen the glory When old comrades get together Like in the good old days So sweep away the pickets and good day to you Doktor Teller chief steppenwolf who stood on guard with warheads & strategies of overkill Bomb now pay later So good night blind flight of black avenging angels (bo-marks of death zeroed on infinity) and good night great mute poets & professors who only stand and wait and good night papa Hemingway who also finked out and good night grandpa Ezra and good night reverend Eliot who also fabricated & abdicated Hurry up please it's time and good night stream of unconscious novelists & non-objecting painters Thou shalt not kill except by complicity and good day Dylan We shall not go gentle into their good night and good day

74

Neruda and good day Ginsberg who saw great heads "draw back weeping" from their plots and good day Fidel He doesn't want to marry your sister He just wants to socialize And good night good night sweet dreams crazy Karl Marx I too wish the state would wither away (into a world without countries & their great draggy nationalisms & their great draggy governments which aren't our idea of communities of love) so good night old old comrades The good old days are gone forever so goodbye goodbye death and good morning sun and goodbye senators and good morning heart that wakes at night & hears itself and good morning crocus voices and good morning waterbirds cawing & cawing and good morning lovers south of 14th street about to turn off the whole evil scene and turn on beautiful & great where the air is green

1962

TELEGRAM FROM SPAIN

NEWS FROM NOWHERE FALSE WAR RECORDS FOUND & LOST INHABI
TANTS CARRYING CHICKENS UNDER ARM BENT COCKS BETWEEN
LEGS STEALING SURVIVAL ORANGES IN ALHAMBRA GARDENS AMONG
INVENTORIES OF WORN-OUT POLITICAL SLOGANS SOWN IN VEGETABLE
GARDENS OF THE GUARDIA CIVIL SLUSHPUMPS GUMMED WITH BLOOD
OF ANOTHER GENERATION CRANKCASES JAMMED WITH NEST OF
FEATHERLESS BIRDS WHOSE BEATING WINGS STILL WON'T MAKE
THE WHEELS TURN BACKWARDS WITH SKELETONS OF STONE LIBERA
TORS FLOWN OFF THE TOPS OF IMITATION MONUMENTS ON GRAND
AVENIDAS DOWN WHICH RUSSIAN TRACTORS ONCE RAN INTO SUGAR
CANE FIELDS BURNING WITH ANARCHISTS AND FUCK YOU CRIED THE
QUEEN WHEN FERDINAND FOUND THE SULTAN IN HIS SACK AND
P.O.U.M! POUM! THE GENERALISSIMO ROSE & SANK FROM SIGHT
UNDER THE WEIGHT OF HIS OWN MEDALS MADE OF MERDE & IRONY
POLITICAL VEGETARIANS FORCED AT LAST TO FEED ON THE GREAT
PORKER HIMSELF & SO THEMSELVES DEVOURED AT LAST BY CEN
TURY PLANTS OF THEIR OWN SOWING

24 Marzo 65

WHERE IS VIETNAM?

Meanwhile back at the Ranch the then President also known as Colonel Cornpone got out a blank Army draft and began to fill in the spaces with men and Colonel Cornpone got down to the bottom of the order where there is a space to indicate just where the troops are to be sent and Colonel Cornpone got a faraway look in his eye and reached out and started spinning a globe of the world and his eye wandered over the spinning surface of the world and after a long time he said I See No Relief so they brought him a relief map of the world and he looked at it a long time and said Thank You Gentlemen I see it all very clearly now yes indeed everything stands out very clearly now and I can see the oceans themselves rolling back and Western Civilization still marching Westward around the world and the New Frontier now truly knows no boundaries and those there Vietnamese don't stand a Chinaman's chance in Hell but still there's all these Chinamen who think they do and also think they can actually reverse the Westward march of civilization and actually reverse the natural Westward spin of our globe but Gentlemen these are not War Games this is not Space Angels this is the real thing Gentlemen and I know right exactly where this here Vietnam is Gentlemen and I want to make doubly sure that all our own people know right exactly where this here Vietnam is Gentlemen in case any of you should happen to get cornered by some eggheads or someone And just then Ladybird came running and Colonel Cornpone stepped into the cloakroom and whispered to her The world really does rotate Westward don't it? and she being smarter than he as is usually the case whispered back that this here Vietnam was not a place but a state of mind and Colonel Cornpone got that old faraway look again and stepped back onto the front porch and sat there rocking for a long time and then said Gentlemen I am a family man and this is for real and I am hereby ordering the complete and final liberation of Vietmind I mean Vietnam for the roots of the trouble are found wherever the landless and oppressed the poor and despised stand before the gates of opportunity and are not allowed across the Frontier into the Great Society which seems to lie out before me like a land of dreams and so Gentlemen here we go fasten your seatbelts we are powerful and free and united there ain't much we can't do and so Gentlemen let me point out to you exactly where it is we all are going on this here globe because Gentlemen even though I am reputed never to have been out of the United States I do know right where we are going on the brink of Vietmind I mean Vietnam and even though we don't want to stop the world spinning in the right direction even for an instant I do want to slow it down just long enough for me to put my finger for you right on this here sore spot which is Vietmine I mean Vietnam and Colonel Cornpone put out his hand to slow down the world just a bit but this world would not be slowed down a bit this world would not stop spinning at all and Texas and Vietnam spun on together faster and faster slipping away under Colonel Cornpone's hand because the surface of this world had suddenly become very very slippery with a strange kind of red liquid that ran on it across all the obscene boundaries and this world went on spinning faster and faster in the same so predestined direction and kept on spinning and spinning and spinning and spinning!

1966

SALUTE

To every animal who eats or shoots his own kind
And every hunter with rifles mounted in pickup trucks
And every private marksman or minuteman
                              with telescopic sight
And every redneck in boots with dogs
                              & sawed-off shotguns
And every Peace Officer with dogs
                              trained to track & kill
And every plainclothesman or undercover agent
                    with shoulderholster full of death
And every servant of the people gunning down people
                    or shooting-to-kill fleeing felons
And every Guardia Civil in any country guarding civilians
                    with handcuffs & carbines
And every border guard at no matter what Check Point Charley
          on no matter which side of which Berlin Wall
                    Bamboo or Tortilla curtain
And every elite statetrooper highwaypatrolman in custom-
          tailored ridingpants & plastic crash helmet
          & shoestring necktie & sixshooter in silver-
          studded holster
And every prowlcar with riotguns & sirens and every riot-tank
          with mace & teargas
And every crackpilot with rockets & napalm underwing
And every skypilot blessing bombers at takeoff
And any State Department of any superstate selling guns
          to both sides
And every Nationalist of no matter what Nation in no matter
          what world Black Brown or White
                              who kills for his Nation

And every prophet or poet with gun or shiv and any enforcer
            of spiritual enlightenment with force and any
            enforcer of the power of any state with Power
And to any and all who kill & kill & kill & kill for Peace
I raise my middle finger
in the only proper salute

Santa Rita Prison, 1968

THE THIRD WORLD

This loud morning
    sensed a small cry in
      the news
         paper
       caught somewhere on
        an inner page
             I
     decide to travel for lunch &
     end up in an automat
           White House Cafeteria
  looking thru a little window
   put a nickle in the slot
    and out comes
          fried rice
Taking a tour
   of the rest of that building
 I hear a small cry
    beyond the rice paddies
      between floors where
        the escalator sticks
and remember last night's dream of
attending my own funeral
   at a drive-in mortuary
   not really believing
      I was that dead
  Someone throwing rice
        All the windows dry
Tipped the coffin open & laughed
          into it
   and out falls
       old funnyface
      myself

                    the bargain tragedian
            with a small cry
followed by sound of Che Guevara singing
        in the voice of Fidel

Far over the Perfume River
                            the clouds pass
            carrying small cries
The monsoon has set in
                    the windows weep

        I
        back up to
                    the Pentagon
    on a flatbed truck
and unload the small brown bodies
                fresh from the blasted fields!

1968

ENIGMA OF HO CHI MINH'S FUNERAL

I am walking down the middle
of Telegraph Avenue Berkeley
in the middle of the surrealist enigma
which is Ho Chi Minh's funeral
Revolution
comes out a thirdstory window
on a recordplayer
Whatever
colors the mind
is a raga
Red Ganges
washes over mine
as water over shallows
When the mode of the music changes
someone throws bathwater out
with a burning baby in it
The People's parade
makes a U-turn
and washes up at the door
of the Free Church
where they hang up Ho's portrait
with red&black flags on the Cross
They are passing out red&green flowers
and reading Ho Chi Minh's Prison Poems
from the pulpit
An old friend I never knew very well
comes up & kisses me
waving her new Black baby
A black tank trundles by
waving its red light
and whining electronically
Back in Genoa Street

Nadja opens the door of her womb
to a great poet
It is illuminated by a very small light bulb
neither black nor red
I stand there reading
a post-revolutionary poem by Yevtushenko
which claims truth is no longer truth
when the Revolution incidentally
sets fire to a loved one's roof
At the corner of Grant & Filbert
another Nadja named Natasha Nevsky
comes to bid me a red-eyed goodbye
on her way to a bed
in the home town of Dostoevsky
I join the parade again
in my red Volkswagen tepee
A very small party of poets joins me
The photo of Ho seems to be saying ho-ho
hollowly
Waving a small black flag
which turns red subsequently
I run over my family
accidentally

1969

LETTER TO A YOUNG POET
IN CUBA OR MAYBE SPAIN

I have just discovered the Nineteen Sixties
in all the places I passed through
and all the trips I took
at the intersection of
the rotten cheese which is Europe
and the Bardo Thodol
in the intersection of
that European darkness not our darkness
and the First-and-last Frontier
which is San Francisco
in the intersection of
Hare Krishna and Kama Sutra
el orgasmo de dios
in the intersection of Quetzalcoatl and Fidel
Shiva and Allen Ginsberg
dancing in eternity
arms around each other
in the intersection of love
and of the Great White Whale stranded
between Charles Olson Jack London and Jack Kerouac
in the intersection of revolution & evolution
between too many turn-ons
and too many far-out trips
in the intersection of
two dreams and two deliriums
Drunken Boat and Sun Ra boat
hashish y bomba de hidrogeno
reino de politico de queso con mierda
I have just discovered the Nineteen Seventies
in the intersection of
the bad breath of modern poetry

and la voce del popolo
as the world sinks deeper & deeper
into the Kali Yuga
There's a high wind blowing
Watch out
when the shit hits the fan
Hummingbird Hummingbird die right on time
But the mind is still the sun
traveling through the sky
And the mind also rises
Abrazos revolucionarios
mis hermanos del Sur

1970

A WORLD AWASH
WITH FASCISM AND FEAR

This land is awash with fascism & fear
And the jails cry for freedom
Let us not deal with the obvious
                    exemplars & assholes of fascism
We will not name them with new free publicity
We all know where certain
                    fat cats are at
        Their medals
                    give them away
We all know where the Party with the capital P
                                            is at
We all know where the People with a capital P
                                        are at
They are in the country and know where
                                    it's at
And the country is rotten with fascism
as the world cries for freedom
There is too much of it
    and not enough of it
        and still we cry for it
            still they cry for it
                and eagles cry
                        America First & Last!
                        My Country, Tears of Thee!
                        And Power to the People!
                    with fists raised fatally
                                as in fascist brigades
                        of the Spanish Civil War
Yes yes the world turns & turns on its fascist axis

And all the old assholes decorated with ribbons
   still sit on the top of the pile
     on top of the heaps of bods and bodies
       who cry to be drawn by Heinrich Kley
      who cry to be drawn by Goya
        who cry to be painted by Daumier
          who cry to be smelted by Rodin-on-fire
the old assholes with their baboon bottoms
     still blowing out the same old snorts of
            Law & order!
           Love Thy Neighbor or Else!
And the animal world cries for freedom
   And the Third World cries for freedom
              and turns itself into a Fourth
          and burns itself
And the Basques cry for freedom
And the Jews cry for freedom
Husbands cry for freedom
   And Women cry for freedom
     And illuminated Heads cry for freedom
      And faggots burn for freedom
        And men are everywhere shut up
And the world rolls on lousy with fascism
  The jails groan with it
    and governments groan with it
And wherever there's a flag with red in it
the people holding it up
              groan with it
          and every flag has red in it
And when they wave it
           it drips blood
          upon them
    The blood falls upon those
       from whom it is bled
         from whom it is wrung

The blood falls upon those
about whom the song is sung
And the world mops it up
And the world rolls on with its
barrels of blood
For this land is our land and is rotten with fascism
of the Left and the Right
not to mention the unsilent Center
not to mention the unsilent subcultures
of uniformed guards
& highwaypatrolmen
& aerospace executives
& the short-haired hyenas
of American big business
not to mention the unsilent undergrounds
of speed & smack & cocaine
and Charles Manson & Hell's Angels into junk
ripping off the world
And there are no ends but means
I weep for you William Fritsch
And this land runneth over with fascism
underground & overground
not to mention Scientology
and its psychic authoritarianism
not to mention one branch of the followers of
Gurdjieff the Baron Munchausen of the mystics
and his psychic authoritarianism
not to mention certain aspects of Synanon
whose Leader must have once read
Hermann Hesse's *Bead Game* and seized upon it
as the perfect model for a self-contained élite
society within a society
with its own hierarchy its own peer groups
and its own compleat morality
not dependent on the Outside World

89

Not to mention certain psychedelic
            marathon encounter groupies
and their psychic authoritarianism
            in the Inside World
Not to mention the Inside-out world
of great non-fascist governments
            which can't exist without supporting
                fascist paradises around the world
Let us not go into that
We all know about the Biggest Brothers
Their names are mouthed every night
            in the jails of Turkey in the jails of Spain
            in the jails of Burgos in the madhouses of nowhere
            in the Women's Houses of Detention
                in the jails of Vincennes
                    in the jails of Moscow and Marin
                        in the jails of Jakarta and the jails
                            of Germany East & West
                    I cannot list all the jails of the world
                            the jails of Greece
                        and the jails of Formosa
                        and the jails of Czechoslovakia & Poland
            yes yes and the jails all the jails of this good old
                            land of the free
where even unions are rank with the file of force
    where even the Boy Scouts of America
        not to mention the American Legion
            is infiltrated with authoritarian fat-asses
            used-car salesmen by day
                national commanders by night
                in overseas caps
                    afraid
        of Expanded Consciousness

where even the radical Left is split
        by Black Cleavers
    suppressing individual freedom
        for revolutionary ends
    And there are no Ends
                        There are only means
                    even when the awful means
                    are awfully justified
                    I weep for you George Jackson
            not to mention this country of ours by the sea
Where National Educational Television
                quakes at the slightest Congressional grumble
            and covers the cutting-room floor
                with the celluloid blood of poet-heads
        for quote artistic reasons unquote
but the clip that falls to the floor
                happens to have the footage
                    of the poet raising his Middle Finger
                    to the President-General
                    And who the fuck is the artist?
            I have only one life to live
            And Whistler's Mother is rocking
For this land is running with fascism & fear
    while the jails cry freedom
                    Men are still chained to rock
                    And Sisyphus cries for help again
                as the Rock rolls back again
                    upon him
as Quentin cries for freedom
    as Soledad cries for freedom
        and felons cry for freedom
            and offer themselves as exchanges
        for American prisoners in North Vietnam
            who are also felons
            and should not be ransomed

for they are the innocent or semi-innocent
or not-so-innocent agents of
rampant national fascisms
with which the world is so sick

as it still cries out

and still cries out

for freedom freedom

freedom

1971

BASEBALL CANTO

Watching baseball
sitting in the sun
eating popcorn
reading Ezra Pound

and wishing Juan Marichal
would hit a hole right through
the Anglo-Saxon tradition
in the First Canto
and demolish the barbarian invaders

When the San Francisco Giants take the field
and everybody stands up to the National Anthem
with some Irish tenor's voice
piped over the loudspeakers
with all the players struck dead in their places
and the white umpires like Irish cops
in their black suits and little black caps
pressed over their hearts
standing straight and still
like at some funeral of a blarney bartender
and all facing East
as if expecting some Great White Hope
or the Founding Fathers
to appear on the horizon
like 1066 or 1776 or all that

But Willie Mays appears instead
in the bottom of the first
and a roar goes up
            as he clouts the first one into the sun
                    and takes off
                            like a footrunner from Thebes

The ball is lost in the sun
and maidens wail after him
but he keeps running
through the Anglo-Saxon epic

And Tito Fuentes comes up
looking like a bullfighter
in his tight pants and small pointed shoes

And the rightfield bleachers go mad
with chicanos & blacks & Brooklyn beerdrinkers
"Sweet Tito! Sock it to heem, Sweet Tito!"
And Sweet Tito puts his foot in the bucket
and smacks one that don't come back at all
and flees around the bases
like he's escaping from the United Fruit Company
as the gringo dollar beats out the Pound
and Sweet Tito beats it out
like he's beating out usury
not to mention fascism and anti-semitism

And Juan Marichal comes up
and the chicano bleachers go loco again
as Juan belts the first fast ball
out of sight
and rounds first and keeps going
and rounds second and rounds third
and keeps going
and hits pay-dirt
to the roars of the grungy populace
As some nut presses the backstage panic button
for the tape-recorded National Anthem again
to save the situation

but it don't stop nobody this time
in their revolution round the loaded white bases
in this last of the great Anglo-Saxon epics
in the *Territorio Libre* of baseball

'The thought of what America would be like'
if the *Cantos* had a wider circulation
'troubles my sleep'

1971

LAS VEGAS TILT

I.

Past the highway sign that reads
                THE FATE OF THE WORLD
                    DEPENDS UPON
                THE WAY WE LIVE:
                SEE SOUTH SAN FRANCISCO
We're into the Big Sky
the whole earth catalog spread below
Day moon flies by
                    like a coin
                flipped into Vegas
Banks of cloud
                whir thru slots
                            of jetstream
        Ding-ding jackpots
                        flush up
                into blue air
Pilots up front
                with Southren accents
            in hidden cab
            pulling slotted levers
A tailwind helps us
                thru a backward hour
            with vodka on the rock
Down down so soon
                    into Vegas
with fear & loathing
                    we drop ding-a-ling
            into it
Help Help

'We are beginning our gradual descent'
down Dante's fire escape
past friendly Bogey at five o'clock
Strike
   the dingbat zone
Tumblers spin
Landscape lights up
And the world registers TILT
We dip down
thru bumpy airpockets
banks of cloud-pinballs
Buffalo Heads
in silverdollar windtunnels
five-and-dime intestines
Touch down
jiggle down on rubber wheels
dolly up to it
in life's slick chariot
of the sun
Judas Iscariot
on the run

II.

Spacecraft Earth spins on
And in the airport
the first slots light up
flashing on & off
     COIN ACCEPTED
 whir whir whir
     INSERT COIN
Indian Head rejects
      fall out the Coin Return
where one-armed masturbators wait

97

Flushed out
          we stagger into it
Landed in desert
               we find no desert
no Nile to float down
               with Voznesensky
but Cleopatra's Barge near Nero's Nook
   with real plastic fish in its pool
          plastic raft to float on
             down Mississippis
   A Moscow poet and an American on it

Where Tom Sawyer?
          Who Huck Finn?
                    Where Injun Jim?

Jesus in dark glasses
on the bus to the Strip
carrying thirty pieces of silver
in a paper bag
In front of him an epileptic
in a gold golf cap
shaking his head continuously
uncontrollably
The silverhaired busdriver starts up
humming a tune from *Naughty Marietta*
We hum past
               Tropicana Avenue   Lone Palm Motel
     Shell Mobil   Private Pool Suites   Looney Tunes
     HEAVEN   Funny Farm   Rent-a-Car   Solarcaine
          Paradise Road Blue Chip Stamps   GOLF
   Ice   Le Cafe   THE END   Drugs   HACIENDA
     Mormon Temple   Towaway Zone   Coppertone
          Gulf   Silver Slipper   Auto Refrigeration
          Progressive Jackpots   Nevada Visitors Bureau

98

```
        Penny Slots & Free Drinks        Las Vegas Boulevard
          Play Nickels Win New Car        Hughes Air West
            Bonanza Casino        Check Cashing Service
        FOLIES BERGERE        "Never Before"        Sage & Sand
              Hunt Breakfast        HOOVER DAM
                  'Old-Fashioned Hospitality'
                        Frontier Hotel
                    LAS  VEGAS  HILTON
                        THE  DUNES
                          STARDUST
                        Westward Ho
                        SHOWBOAT
                         FLAMINGO
                        DESERT  INN
                         PYRAMIDS
                      CAESAR'S  PALACE
                        Orange Julius
                      Our Marriage Chapel
                    Little Church of the West
                     'Thirty Dollar Weddings'
                   'Go Home Satisfied or Refund'
```

Jesus Christ Superstar gets off

'Everyman, I'll go with thee
and be thy guide
In thy most need to go
by thy side'

III.

The end of the American dream
begins again
on the Street That Never Sleeps

And 'the extraordinary adventure of white America'
roars on
amid the proofs it never experienced the Middle Ages
A huge cowboy on a hundred-foot horse
sits astride main street downtown
raises his neon Stetson
and says electronically
                    'Howdy, pardner'
His voice fills the air
                    his voice is everywhere
                    his picture printed in
                        The Voice of the Rockies
                            in the *Desert News*
                                with his daily horoscope:
'Scorpions are mystery men, violent and volcanic inside, de-
ceptively cool outside. They believe in revenge and vigorous
pursuit of women. The women among them make good spies,
the men good Mafia dons or police officers, either way, and
superb athletes. Let not Aries enter these premises.'

Desert News sifts in like sand:
            CLEVELAND MAFIA RULES VEGAS
                'Geologists Say No Vegas Fault'
            'Hearst's Daughter Castigates Hearst's America
                Attacks "Absolute Spiritual Bankruptcy" '
        'People change in Vegas and become what they would like
            to become and what they can't become back home'
                    'Who Is Not on the Hustle
                        In Life's Lottery?'
A covy of Oklahoma Mothers
with cowboy escorts
lands in The Blue Lagoon
A honeymoon couple from North Duluth
parks their blue Ford Phaeton
and struggles to the slots

100

Lady in lobby in powderblue pants & clogs
sprays her hair with a blue spray can
talking on a lobby phone
      'We come down here to a land sale.
       We dint buy no land
        but they give us free tickets
        to everything!'
A Japanese student with a skin problem
and a camera
scurries past to the john
An Indian with a skin problem
and a turban
is having trouble with his zipper
Slots whir in the Men's Room
         PRESS BUTTON TO FLUSH
And out come the coins or condoms
A minister in blue
with no skin condition
walks by jingling
a pocketful of dimes
Stands up to a slot
jiggles his pants
presses a button
and drowns

IV.

      ELECTRONIC SHOOTING GALLERY
       in the 'Circus Circus':
      'Shoot the Red Dot'
    'You're in the heart
        of the deepest and darkest
           jungles of Africa—
       Step up
           to the shooting counter, hunters—

pick up a gun, put a quarter in
the slot in front of you
and take careful aim—'

'All the animals you hit
will scream, yell, move or holler—
Take your time
and hit all the red dots—

'Come in, hunters,
if you're brave enough to face
the dangers of the jungle,
pick up a gun
put a quarter in the slot
and start shooting—

'A deadly jungle killer
the black python
is hanging from a tree
waiting for someone
to make *the wrong move*—

'Watch the animals perform—
Pick up a gun
and let them have it—
You get fifteen shots—

'On your left you see a native
with a blowgun—
When he's aiming at you
shoot him—

'You're in the heart
of the deepest and darkest
jungles of Africa—'

```
KLEAN OUT KIKES
    KLEAN OUT WOPS
        KLEAN OUT REDSKINS
        KLEAN OUT SPICS
            KLEAN OUT CREEPS
                KLEAN OUT FREAKS
                    KLEAN OUT BLACK TRASH
(GEORGE JACKSON LIVES)
```

'There once was a man
who sold the Lion's skin
while the beast still lived
and was killed
while hunting him'

V.

L'heure bleue
on the Strip
where time does not exist
except on the wrist of the dealer
and all that glisters is not gelt
and 'behind the tinsel is the real tinsel'
in a Monopoly Game fantasy
dreamed up maybe by some Mormon Moloch
during the Great Depression
                and stretched out there
            in the great American desert
        like some portable instant city
    set down on the face of another planet
        A five-mile long strip of gyzm
    squeezed out like dry toothpaste on a cake

In desert dust storms
   tumbleweeds
          still blow
      across Las Vegas Boulevard
           and still will blow
         after a river runs thru
        Caesar's parkinglot
      with its cargo of dead cars

The Strip lights up
           like a pinball machine
  or a linear accelerator
        brighter than the moon up close
    the sky a neon ceiling
          for a room inside a lightbulb
  where it does no good to close your eyes

A helicopter from the Stardust Casino
                moves the stars about
     over the Appian Way
    And the Roman legions come rolling
      like a Rose Bowl Parade
    with Caesar's Great Triumphal Car
      drawn by six Percherons
         hung with elephant bells
   and leading Dürer's Rhinoceros
             on a string

There is a thrill in the air
The Roman legions come rolling
          up to Caesar's Palace
Centurions
     swing off their horseless chariots
       parade up thru the gates
     come to a halt & raise their visors
        And look about

The face of the pit boss stares out
chewing the butt end
of a burned-out Havana
He raises his right arm
holds it like a salute
and brings it down with a crash
There is a whirring sound
His eyes light up and spin
with dollar signs in them

VI.

Like a lost plane
with feathered wings
The Winged Victory of Samothrace
has landed somehow
in front of
CAESAR'S PALACE
built by building trades
with union funds
Martial's Palatine Sonnet
quoted in the menu
And 'Room Service a Roman Feast'
in the Frank Sinatra Suite
but no food served with Harry Belafonte
at the Midnight Supper Show
designed precisely to disgorge
the lushed-up masses
directly into the
carrousel Casino
groaning with gaming tables
Roulette Baccarat Keno
in a sea of slotmachines

one of which once in a while lights up
shakes all over
showers out Caesar's own silverdollars
and emits a puff of smoke
Whiskey America plunges in
into the Soft Machine
into the steaming pits
as into a scene from Dante
painted by Gustav Doré
whose clouds were angels
Caesar not Virgil thy guide

Wearing blue and carrying a feather
will not win
Belafonte himself falls in
and drops $27,000
at Baccarat
and next night sings a song-cry
about the pit bosses:
'If it moves and is warm
I will fleece it'
And all that glisters
is not guilt
at the baccarat tables
two dealers deal
the final Big Brother trip
And two pit bosses watch them
and three foremen watch the pit bosses
and one pit boss watches three foremen
from behind two-way mirrors
on the low ceiling
under which circulate the masses
mixed with house-dicks

Hoc in terra Caesar est

The pudgy pit boss squats
                    on his highchair throne
    rings on fat fingers
                and a fat cigar clutched loose
a De Mille Caesar
            with lizard looks watching wrong moves
 Drear players with coin-eyes
                stuck like horned toad zombies
                round the board
    'Phlebas the Phoenician a fortnight dead'
        holds his cards and hangs his head
 Dawn breaks outside somewhere
                    and the deal continues
Gold sun bursts forth unseen somewhere
                through a cottonwood grove
    And the big shuffle goes on
    The walls themselves fall down
                    as in Buster Keaton movies
        and they still play on
                Pale Faces turning paler
            impaled on rotating spits in pits
            roasted with rotating oranges
                apples & cherries
                under glass
            through which also wink & blink
            Buffalo Heads & Indian Heads
    in hock in terror   in bas-relief
        And Eisenhower eyes and Kennedy eyes
        And the weird Third Eye that winks not
            from its Transamerica Pyramid
            in the dollar's
                    green desert
    upon which hangs a sign
                    WE NEVER CLOSE

VII.

And now at Angels Peak in morning light
thirty miles above Vegas
Andrei Voznesensky asks no quarter
but takes a coin of his own
and drops it in the mouth of the daughter
of the President of Caesar's Palace
and pulls her right arm down
and waits for the virgin coin
to fall out below
if he's that lucky

And at Indian Rock Refuge
we get out
and climb up the steep riprap
to the Indian cave at the top
from which the flat world can be seen
and drop small round flat stones
into slots in it

And await the final
deluge jackpot landslide
of earth and life

in which the fate of the world
depends upon
the way we live

1971

FORTY ODD QUESTIONS
FOR THE GREEK REGIME
AND ONE CRY FOR FREEDOM

Can you tell me the way to the American Express?

Can you show me the way to a real Greek taverna filled with picturesque dancing descendants of the first democracy on earth?

Where do we catch the boat for Plato's Republic?

Is it true that your great Greek tragedies and tragi-comedies are now being performed daily in police stations?

Where is Katsimbalis Where Zorba Who stole Euripides?

Is it true the Victory of Samothrace turned to turds April Twenty-first?

Why did you steal the Elgin Marbles?

Have you ever looked into Chapman's Homer?

What have you done with my island?

Are you a bunch of smart guys putting us on or imbeciles who really mean it?

What have you done with the young poets in small boats and the old poets on bicycles?

How are things in the torture chambers of Bouboulina Street?

Did you know Jacqueline Onassis once was married to a democrat you would have liked to torture?

Why is there not room in Greece for the grave of one more free man?

Who moved the Trojan Horse to Athens?

Will Aphrodite ever find her arms?

Where is the light of Greece, the violet light of Attica?

Why can't we just sail away to the Isles of Greece and forget everything?

Why did the King cut out so fast, with his suitcases, his little dogs, and his great mother?

Why isn't the Constitution printed on a rope?

Have you seen Ulysses' dog lately with all his eyes on you?

Why can't I drink retsina lately without getting more thirsty?

Why hasn't the Oracle of Delphi spoken out lately?

How come more American poets don't attack you?

Why won't you just Go Away if we ignore you?

Where is the light of Greece, the violet light of Attica?

Is it true you'll screw anything that moves even on Sunday?

Why isn't your Constitution printed on money?

Who will rescue the phoenix from the fascist soldiers that spring out of its flames on every matchbox signpost and mailbox?

Can you still hear the cocks of Athens crow from the Acropolis?

Do you know what they're crying?

Where is the light of Greece, the violet light of Attica?

Can you still read Greek?

Does "Z-Z-Z-Z-Z-Z" mean the sound of sleep to you?

Does "Z-Z-Z-Z" make you think we're sleeping?

Does *Zoë* still mean Life in your language?

Does *Zei* still mean "He lives" in your language?

Do you think *Elefteria* means Leftover Freedom?

Have you forgotten the word for Liberty?

Can your tongue still pronounce it?

We still can still announce it

Elefteria agapi mou!

First read at a benefit for the Greek Resistance, Fugazi Hall, San Francisco, April 20, 1972

CARNAVAL DE MAÏZ

In the churches of Cholula
                    the bleeding Christs groan
                        their Indian misericordias
        as Christian saints in cages
            wring their wood hands
                over bloodblack rosaries
            wailing & bewailing
                            Great God Death
                    in Churrigeuresque chapels
                    wherein sweet Indian faces
                    had their burro-vision bent
                        into 'Heaven-sent'
                        baroque monstrosities
White Christ Quetzalcoatl was predicted
        and did indeed land
            and did indeed take that land in pawn
And still riseth up ruined & raunchy
        with barbaric yawn
            in the dawn of a new debacle
As we walk into it chewing chicle
                carrying cameras & Oaxaca blankets
And also groan aloud
                        but only for
                            what we would ignore
And still hold our breath
                    and tread with stealth
            among the wealth of what we call
                            'medieval superstition'
As we in Norteamerica now
                    have indeed abolished Death
        and no longer need
                    such monuments & consolations

We have banned it forever from our lives
                    and seldom see anyone dying anymore
                              except on TV in some foreign country
          And freeze our bodies to unthaw uncancered
                    a thousand years hence
          And decay and dissolution
                              have no sight of us
          who are in effect immortal
Only the gods lie & die in us
And still *La Patria es primera*
                    all over this divided earth
          where the poor will be born without ass-holes
                    if shit should ever become valuable
                    And they stay stuck in the ground forever
in that ground which is graded & regraded
                                   traded and retraded
                                   deeded & misdeeded
                                             all over Mesoamerica
where every revolution still
                         boils down to the scam
          of 'getting land without men
                         for men without land'
          who will still spring up
                    like teeth on ears of corn
in the hands of that International Harvester
          whose mouth unsinging
                         ever hangeth open
          avaricious
                    and slobbering!

11 Mayo 72

ALASKA PIPE DREAM

One fine day like the day after tomorrow while the Canadian Energy Minister was minding his own business by saying the Alaska Oil Pipeline was really an 'internal matter' in the USA and not for Canadians to jump into, one fine day in the not very distant future while the Energy Minister was talking he suddenly noticed that one leg of his trousers was wet, and hoping it was not what he thought it was, having for some time been housebroken, he reached down and determined that in fact it was not an internal matter at all but an external matter of oil, and yet not pure oil for when he inspected his hand he found it not only oily but bloody, and when he rushed to the lab to find out why blood was mixed with oil and whether or not it was *his* blood mixed with *their* oil or *their* blood mixed with *his* oil or whatever, he was informed by the lab hired by the oil company that there was really nothing to worry about at all, since the blood would not stop the oil from working perfectly in American war machines and automobiles, not to mention the Mayor of Montreal's Ford, and in any case the blood was not the Canadian ministry's blood and it was not the American people's blood, it was simply the blood of one billion waterfowl who had been unable to feed in the tundra which had been disrupted by the perfectly innocent Pipeline, and it was simply the blood of one billion fish in Canadian waterways and one billion fish in Canadian seaways who were no longer able to eat the plankton now flavoured with salted oil, and it was simply the blood of one billion deer in the Northern Territory and one billion other wild animals in other frozen territories in the Siberia of Canada which had gradually become unfrozen for the first time in recorded time due to the world's largest Oil Spill which had resulted from earthquake Pipeline rupturings which caused a great wash of hot underground oil to pour Eastward from

Alaska all over the geologic underground strataface of Canada, so that the St. Lawrence dripped both oil and animal blood into the water supply of the City of Montreal, but this was strictly an Internal American Matter, and we were not concerned at all, at all. . . .

Montreal, March 1973

American Mantra & Songs

Interested in developing chants with American English words as opposed to singing Sanskrit or other unknown tongues, I at one time or another sang spoke or chanted these verses in varying versions, sometimes with much spontaneous repetition not herein noted, often with autoharp accompaniment.

MOTHER OF LIGHT MANTRA

Father of love

        Mother of rain

Father of night

        Mother of pain

Father of day

        Mother of light

Mother of phantoms

        Mother of phantoms

Dark ages over now

Dark ages over now

Dark old daddy

Father of phantoms

Mother of light

Dark ages over now

Dark old daddy

Rainman dance and sing!

(*After Zimmerman*)

BIG SUR SUN SUTRA

Sun Sun

Ah sun Om sun

Sun Sun Sun

Great God Sun

Still riseth in our Rubaiyat

and strikes and strikes

And strikes the towers

with a shaft of light!

Strikes us in our Sun-ra boat

Strikes and strikes us in our Sun-ra boat

Sun Light Life Light

Sun Sun Sun

Great God Sun!

LAUGHING & CRYING

I laugh to hear me say what I am saying

Walking in my cave of flesh

There must be a place

There must be a place

Where all is light

I laugh to hear me say what I am saying

O Rama

Audiart O Audiart

dancing Shiva dear one

Your face flies through the sky

I laugh to say what I am saying

Each of us a lamp

a spirit-lamp

a lantern burning

a lamp a place beyond a turning

where all is light

I laugh and cry

with mask of tears

and laughing face

I laugh and cry to hear me say what I am saying

My laughing face

and mask of tears

makes me laugh and cry to hear me sing what I am saying

For there must be a place

There must be a place

where all is light

NIGHT LIGHT

Night, night

Death's true self, Death's second self

Black is my true love's hair

Yet all, all is despair

Black night, black light

Death's true self

Black, black, black is my true love's hair

And all, all is despair

Night, night

Death's second self

where all is empty, all is despair

All gone, all down

All, all despair

And grey is my true love's hair

Yet sun bursts forth upon the land

And a butterfly lights in it

upon my hand

And lights these songs

and lights these songs

in air

TANTRIC BALLAD

Man and woman meet and part

coupling with their counterpart

in the calyx of the lotus

And the lotus opens and opens

its very heart of light

Lovely lotus opens, opens

and then closes

into night

Man and woman meet and part

coupling with their counterpart

in the calyx of the lotus

which can only close when it opens

which can only open when it closes

Man and woman meet and part

And dear friends die

And night is where our lovers lie

And light is where our lovers lie

in the calyx of the lotus

which opens and opens

and closes and closes

when we live

and when we die

IDOL CHANT

Idol whose feet have golden rubies on them

That golden person who is seen

within the sun

with golden mouth and golden hair

Idol whose feet have golden rubies on them

whose eyes are like blue lotuses

Golden altogether

White light of sun

and blue exceeding darkness

Idol whose feet have golden rubies on them

speak O speak

'the full account of Om'

(After Upanishads, Prapathanka, Kanda 8)

GREAT CHAIN CHANT

Great chain of being Great chain turning

O cycle made of meat

O snake who eats its tail

Great chain of being Great chain turning

O snake who eats its tail

O hungry self

without an end or a beginning

Great chain of being Great chain turning

O hungry self

O wheel of meat

made of us

Great chain of Being

with no end and no beginning

All beings being one

Turn & turn & turn!

AIRPORT MANTRA

(Seeing Allen Ginsberg off to India)

Plane says Om

Sky says Om

Sun says Om Om

When will America sing it

When will America utter it

Om is He who is meat & air

Om is She who is Light

Om is universe spinning

Sound of universe singing

Love-sound of Om

Sigh-cry of Om

Mutter and moan of Om Om

Breath of life which is Om

Om America unknown

singeth in the void

SPONTANEOUS ANARCHIST
PACIFIST BUDDHIST SONG

(To be delivered in the Russian heroic style)

War! War! War!

World! World! World!

Life, Light, Love, Men & Women!

All one

One boat of meat!

Rock rock rock!

Past Present Future All time All one

All places planets things & beings one

All color sound and taste and touch

all one

All form and emptiness

All living entities All sentient beings one

Old Age Annihilation Death & Suffering

All Sensation Thought & Tears & Laughter

Ecstasy

Sweet dear words Sweet caresses too

All one

All Light All made of Light

One breathing Universe

Highest Perfect Wisdom breathing

All poems & songs

All lips & tongues & voices One

Mystic texts of our bodies

make love not war!

(After The Great Paramita Sutra)

NINE SHAMAN SONGS RESUNG

(Upon Last Looking into Arthur Waley's Translation of 'The Nine Songs')

I.

Strike the Dark Strings

Strike Strike

the dark strings

And reed & zither answer

Spirit moves

in splendid gear

And is the body's splendid shaman

through which a god may sing

And indeed does sing

And strikes and strikes

that Darkest Bell

ah darkest bell—

my body struck

with love

II.

Flower-spirit, shaman-child

in blaze of brightness dancing

Endless as the earth

She dances round it

As sun

As mantic moon

in dragon-chariot of sun

O endless flight!

Part of me climbs to heaven

through the four seas & seasons

Longing for you

III.

She-shaman princess

               in a stone boat

      in winged dragon-boat

                  awning of fig-vine

         sweet flag paddles

             magnolia rudder

Rides to that Island

         to that Bright Island

              abode of light

     Swinging her mesmere lamp

         her incense burner

              on a gold chain

      She drops her thumb-ring in the Sea

And turning

     and turning

           stretches her body burning

                   toward me

(though she told me told me

she was not

free)

And flying dragons sweep her far away

from me

I gallop my horse in the morning

through the lowlands by the river

IV.

I build a bride-room

            underwater

      roof thatched with lotus

          courtyard paved with murex

At dark dusk I cross

             to the Western bank

   Here it was

        she cast down

              her thin dress

            upon the shore

Over the white nut grass

          my eyes wander

      see only water swirl

          in the flood rains

Someone says my loved one sent for me

I gallop my horses

              over the lotus leaves

    toward where a dragon waits

            toward where an elk browses

On the Mountain of Nine Doubts

V.

Lord Sun

wheels in flight

trailing his spirit-garment

High over the Nine Hills

          he handles Yin & Yang

male & female

          shade & sunshine

soul & body

          a Yin for every Yang

And gallops into Light

I pluck the lovely hemp flower

      Age creeps on apace

      Soon all will be over

          Soon all done all one

And fate is fixed in the heart

And not to draw nearer

      is to drift forever

            further apart

VI.

Hall full of lovely ones

Yet you had eyes for me alone

Riding a whirlwind A cloud for a banner

Suddenly you came

And as suddenly departed

And only had eyes for me

I bathed with you

in the Pool of Heaven

In a sunny fold of the hill

I dried your hair

Now it is I who shout & sing with despair

Under a chariot-awning

of peacock feathers & halcyon flags

You climb again to the Nine Heavens

VII.

A glow in the sky

        and soon you'll arise

Night pales

        Day shines forth

You ride on thunder wheels

           cloud banners trailing

  heave great sighs

         look back yearning

        for earth's beauty burning

  look and linger

        forget your way

I draw a long arrow

        and shoot Heaven's Wolf

then draw me down the Dipper

        And plunge alone into

          the White Void

VIII.

With you wandered

        down rivers and coasts

  River God

      in fish-scale boat

    drawn by dragons

        with griffin oarsmen

With you I wander

      on the river islands

  go with you as far

       as the Southern Shore

Dark dusk falling

And I too sad

     to think of returning

  Eyes only for

      that farthest shore

  I lie awake

      yearning

IX.

Mountain Spirit left me alone

                  dark in a bamboo grove

Air dark with rain

                  Monkeys twitter again

      cry all night again

               And cry and cry

                  all night again

Waiting for you

              I wander and linger

      turn and turn

            and turn again—

And won't turn back

            and won't turn back—

Without my beloved

STREETS OF SAN FRANCISCO

'Streets of Paris pray for me'

Streets of San Francisco wait for me

Streets in rain and streets in pain

Streets in sin and streets in sun

Streets of Paris Streets of San Francisco

pray for

wait for me

Sun on beaches Sun on mesas

shine on me

rain on rivers

wash me away

Plain tree plain tree

shade me

River of thinking

        drown me drinking

   river of drinking

        drown me thinking

   rain on ocean

        wash me away

Sun on Sunday

        warm and dry me

   moon on Monday

        darkly light me

   lightly light me

        light my way. . . .

(After Palinarus)

BALLAD OF THE BOAT-KEEPER

(In a Brechtian mode)

Last night at midnight

Some people came along the dock

                     laughing and talking

Only one of them was saying

    'Life, life is a fucking tragedy—

    And I come to that conclusion

    as an optimist—'

'No, no,' said another, laughing.

But the first went on:

    'Life is a bloody blood-bath for sure,

    And we are all washed in it—'

'No, no!' said another, laughing.

But the first went on:

    'We sleep in blankets of blood

    And we swim in it

    And all goes down!'

'No, No!' said another, laughing,

And she sang a sweet melody.

But the first went on:

    'Yes, yes, all, all goes down,

    And you too will founder—'

'No, No,' said another, laughing,

'I'll never drown,

I'll never go down,

My life not end, in weeping—'

And his voice died away

        on the Bay

And his voice died away

        in my sleep

And his voice died away

    And his voice died away

        died away

          died away

And his voice and his self

        died away

New Directions Paperbooks

Complete descriptive catalog available free on request from
New Directions, 333 Sixth Avenue, New York 10014.   † Bilingual.